KING CHARLES SPANIELS

This, the only book dealing solely with the King Charles Spaniel, has been specially written for all those many admirers who have waited so long for a book devoted to their own breed.

The King Charles, so popular during the Edwardian era, suffered a decline in popularity right up to the advent of the Second World War. This trend is today happily reversed, and these gay and strikingly handsome dogs are once again showing a marked return to favour.

The author, an acknowledged authority and breeder for very many years has written a book which every King Charles lover, whether owner, would-be owner or breeder will want to possess.

General Editor: CHRISTINA FOYLE

KING
CHARLES
SPANIELS

by

M. Joyce Birchall

FOYLES HANDBOOKS
LONDON

ISBN 0 7071 0612 5

© W. & G. Foyle Ltd. 1960

First published 1960
Reprinted 1970
Reprinted 1973
Reprinted 1976
Revised edition 1977
Reprinted 1982

Published in Great Britain by
W. & G. Foyle Ltd.,
125 Charing Cross Road,
London, WC2H 0EB

Printed and bound in Great Britain
at The Pitman Press, Bath

Dedication

*This book is offered with
humility to all 'Charlie' lovers
the world over*

Acknowledgements are due to the Kennel Club for their permission to reprint the Standard of the Breed and for compiling the list of post-war Champions.

Contents

List of Illustrations

Introduction

IT GIVES ME great pleasure to write an Introduction to this book which the author has taken so much trouble to compile. I hope it will fill a long felt want for a book on the breed to help the novice in particular, who intends to keep a King Charles and wishes to know how to look after it to the best advantage in all ways. At the same time it should be of help to even the older breeders and exhibitors with its pedigrees and lines leading back to the older dogs, as it is the only publication of its kind concerning the breed published in England and offered to the public today.

FLORENCE MITCHELL
Tunbridge Wells.

ONE

A Short History of the Breed

WHAT A galaxy of splendours the very name inspires. These little dogs – so human – are the true aristocrats of the dog world.

The true origin of the King Charles is lost in obscurity. Lady Wentworth, the late President of the King Charles Spaniel Club, spent many years in research on the subject, but even so was unable to come to any concrete conclusions.

The first written reference to the breed in England seems to have been made about 1570. Dr. Caius, Physician to Queen Elizabeth, makes mention of these little dogs as ' the Comforters or Gentle Spaniel ', kept by the Court ladies, as being very useful foot-warmers sitting beneath the voluminous skirts of the period on the owner's feet, or lying against the body – a most useful form of collecting insects in less hygienic periods than our own. The main colours at this time were the Red and White Spaniel (believed to have come from Italy) the Black and White Holland Spaniel, and an all black. The appearance of the spaniel was very different from the modern dog, and paintings show that he resembled more closely the tiny drop-eared Papillon rarely seen nowadays; the muzzle being pointed, the ears and legs well feathered, and the tail long and carried very gaily. The painting of Louis XIV and Family (Wallace Collection) shows a very good example of the type. The Maltese, Pug, and Pomeranian, although not as we know them today, were also known at this time, and it is understandable that old references to the Court pets could show some confusion. It should also be appreciated that there must have been some unauthorised interbreeding between these varieties, which would change and add to each breed.

The next reference to what was possibly a King Charles Spaniel was made about 1587. After the execution of Mary, Queen of Scots, at Fotheringay Castle, a tiny spaniel was found hidden in her clothing and soaked with blood. Nothing further is recorded than that it was taken away and washed.

It was during the reign of the two Charles's, from 1625 to 1685, that the spaniel really came into prominence. Charles I, one of England's greatest beneficiaries to the world of art, appreciated the qualities of these exquisite little dogs, and had some at his Court. His son, Charles II, gave his name to the breed. Mr. Pepys in his diary tells us the palace was full of them, and the King could be seen walking in St. James's Park, followed by his red and white, black and white, and black curly-coated little spaniels (the tan being introduced at a later date by crossing with the Pyrame, a small black and tan webbed-toed water-spaniel with a straight coat).

Henrietta, Charles II's sister and married to Monsieur, the French King's brother, was a great admirer of these little dogs, and possibly brought some over with her from France when visiting her brother.

In 1685, Charles II's brother, James II, was also an admirer of the breed and kept some at Court. William III it is thought might have brought over the Black and White

Holland Spaniel in 1688. These appear to have been introduced previously by Anne of Cleeves. The Duke of Marlborough may also have brought some, eventually crossing them with the Springer (at that time a small dog) and so producing the Marlborough Spaniel.

The Tricolour is fairly certain to have appeared with the crossing of the three colours, that is – the Red and White (Italian Spaniel), Black and White (Holland Spaniel), and the Black.

The year 1828 brings the first mention of a Ruby, though a Van Dyck painting of Phillipe le Roy, two hundred years earlier, shows a red spaniel, with white on head and toes. The Tricolour (Prince Charles) we know today, was a result of crossing Black and Tan with Blenheims, and again breeding the mismarked Black and Tan result back to a Blenheim. The Ruby must also have appeared in this way, first as a mismarked Ruby, then bred back to a Black and Tan, and so eventually breeding true, as did the Tricolour.

Mention of the short-nosed type is first made in 1845, and in 1859 *The Field* reports ' The King Charles and Blenheim Spaniels as bred by the fancy, are snub-nosed, round-headed animals like Pugs, with silky ears and coats, but they are truly graceful animals '. It is considered generally that a bull-dog cross gave the flat face; some, however, contend this was due to the Pug or Japanese crossing.

The King Charles Spaniel enjoyed immense popularity during the Edwardian reign but this gradually declined up to the Second World War, when many spaniels were put down for fear of raids as well as feeding problems. One or two breeders kept going on a smaller scale, and it is from these lines that today's dogs have descended.

The King Charles Spaniel is the companion *par excellence*; once owned, few other dogs satisfy. They are seen at their best running freely in the garden and home, where their quick elegant movements show to advantage. Gaiety, sweetness of temper and undying devotion to their owner are the hall-marks of these enchanting little dogs.

TWO

The Standard of the Breed

THE STANDARD is compiled by the Breed Representative of the Kennel Club Liaison Council, and Officials and Committees of the Breed Specialist Clubs. The Standard being a description of the ideal King Charles Spaniel and is as follows:

GENERAL APPEARANCE
Compact and cobby, on refined lines, chest wide and deep, legs short and straight, back short and level, tail well flagged and not carried over the level of the back. Movement free, active and elegant.

HEAD AND SKULL
Skull massive in comparison to size, well-domed, and full over the eyes. Nose black with large wide open nostrils, very short and turned up to meet the skull. The stop between skull and nose should be well defined. Jaw; muzzle square, wide and deep and well turned up, lower jaw wide, lips exactly meeting giving a nice finish. The cheeks should not fall away under the eyes, but be well cushioned up. A protruding tongue is objectionable, but does not disqualify.

EYES

Very large and dark, set wide apart, with eyelids block square to face line, and with pleasing expression.

EARS

Set on low, and to hang quite flat to cheeks, very long and well feathered.

COAT

Long, silky and straight. A slight wave allowed, not curly. The legs, ears and tail should be profusely feathered.

COLOUR

Black and Tan: A rich glossy black, with bright mahogany tan markings, on muzzle, legs, chest, linings of ears, under tail, and spots over the eyes. *Tricolour*: Ground pearly white and well distributed black patches, brilliant tan markings on cheeks, linings of ears, under tail, and spots over the eyes. A wide white blaze between the eyes and up the forehead. *Blenheim*: A ground of pearly white with well distributed chestnut red patches. A wide clear blaze with the 'spot' in centre of skull. The spot should be a clear chestnut red mark about the size of a sixpence in the centre of skull. *Ruby*: Whole coloured, a rich chestnut red.

WEIGHT AND SIZE

The most desirable size is six to twelve pounds.

FAULTS

The presence of a few white hairs on the chest of a Black and Tan or Ruby is undesirable, but a white patch is a major fault.

* * *

Having studied the Standard, what does the ideal dog look like? To comply with cobbiness a dog must have a rounded rib, a deep brisket, and above all a short level back. The ideal body viewed from the side would be one which measured the same from ground to shoulder, as from the top of the shoulder to the root of the tail. A long cast body detracts immediately from this ideal, and is seen far too often today, and however attractive these specimens are it is going away from the Standard. We have in mind this lovely well-sprung, short-backed little body which is carried between four legs, which must give free active and elegant movement. To do this the construction of the limbs must be perfect. Perfect action once seen is never forgotten. The steps are small but incredibly quick, giving a general impression of lightness, and ease, and an overall impression of great elegance. The forelegs should be straight, well-boned to pasterns, set into a well laid shoulder, and must not be out at elbow, nor placed under the body; the hind-legs, with well muscled thighs, nicely bent at stifle, hocks bent, neither turned in nor out. If the dog is perfectly built in limbs, the hindlegs will have the correct impetus for covering the ground smoothly, and together with the good forelegs will complete the movement picture. A straight stifle – a common fault – although active will give a stiff bustling movement; lack of muscle causing the patella to slip in and out of the socket, will give a lame action; a straight shoulder will give an effect of goose-stepping, a jerky action and quite wrong. Although the King Charles is a Toy dog, efforts should be made to improve action; the patella disease is a breed problem, and not just a post-war one. Much can be done by breeding from stock good in this point.

There are two types of foot in the breed, a round cat-shaped foot with well-cushioned pads, and a foot with the central pads joined and the nails fused together; this in no way inconveniences the dog or its action. This foot would appear to be an inheritance from the Pyrame outcross.

To complete the body picture we must add the tail. The length of the tail varies from breeder to breeder and every puppy must be treated as an individual and docked accordingly. A short backed dog can carry a longer tail than a long backed one; the tail should be carried gaily.

The neck should rise proudly from between the shoulders, bearing one of the most enchanting and intelligent heads a dog could have. There are few heads today that fully conform to the standard; a domed head will automatically be full over the eyes, as the definition of a dome is a half sphere. The dome of St. Paul's Cathedral gives a quick mental picture, and from whatever angle a dome is viewed, it will always be a half-sphere, hence the standard 'well domed and full over the eyes'. Viewed full face the curve will rise between the ears, and side view will rise from the stop to the base of the skull. The majority of skulls today slope away from the stop to base of head, which is immediately detected side view, and too many heads viewed full face are flat headed.

The 'stop', being the indentation between the eyes in the perfect head, should be well-defined and deep, so that the tip of the little finger can fit into the hollow. The nose must be black in all colours, with wide nostrils, very short and turned up towards the skull. The nose completely buried in the skull as in the Pekingese is incorrect, as the standard demands a 'stop'.

In the perfect head the eyes will be large and dark, full of gentleness, and set wide apart square into the head (the small, or light, or obliquely set eye loses the soft, sweet expression, so much a characteristic of the breed; a light eye gives a hard expression, besides being extremely difficult to breed out). The top of the nose should be in a line with the eyes, and the resulting muzzle in this perfect head will be a wide soft curve, beautifully cushioned up under the eyes with a perfect finish to the mouth, the lips just touching, no protruding lower jaw, no pendulous overhanging lips, wry mouths or popping tongues.

The ears must be set a little above the eye-line and to the side of the head; the ears are wide at the root, and the leathers long and thin lying close to the side of the face and heavily fringed. Ear placement can change completely the shape of a skull; set too high a good skull can be made to look almost flat.

Finally, to complete the ideal King Charles, the perfect coat is required, often lacking today; too often it is of a cotton-wool texture instead of the long silky texture so desired. Coats have to be bred for, but grooming can help poor coats as well as make the good one glamorous; the Black and Tans and the Rubys, without the correct quality coats, lack the gloss and lacquered effects the correct textures have.

The importance of coat and fringes on ears, legs and feet cannot be too strongly emphasised; they are as much the inheritance of the King Charles as any other part.

There is considerable variation in weight; size is, I think, of less importance than quality and soundness, the 'ideal' in any size must be the breeder's aim.

THREE

Choosing a Puppy

WHENEVER POSSIBLE visit the kennel where you intend to purchase; have an open mind about colour, it would be a pity to turn down a good puppy because you had set your mind on a different colour. Make it quite clear which you want, a dog or bitch.

A reliable breeder will show you all the puppies available, and both parents if owned by the kennel, with possibly a grandparent; this will give you an opportunity to see how the puppy you choose will turn out. The puppy's breeding or pedigree will be explained to you and possibly photographs may be available of a dominant dog or dogs behind it.

One word of caution: before picking up puppies, do ask the owner's permission. Puppies are surprisingly strong and wriggly in strange hands, and could be permanently injured falling from a height.

If one or two puppies are brought to show visitors, there is usually one who will appeal more than any other for various reasons. Having seen one you like, ask the breeder's opinion; a three-month-old puppy, if well reared, will have good bone, wide chest, nice cobby little body with a rounded rib which will give the right finish. A narrow-looking puppy will in all probability finish up flat-sided and long-backed. The puppy should have a nice straight front and firm hind action; a puppy at three months will need to tighten up in shoulder, but the elbows should not be thrown out when standing naturally if the shoulders are correctly laid; hind action should be free and strong. The skin should be clean and healthy, there is no excuse for lice or fleas, it merely shows the dogs are not properly cared for. A louse-infected puppy is quickly discovered; the skin of the puppy when explored by the fingers, will have a collection of small scabs on its body, especially in the warm parts, chest, neck, armpits, tail root and ears, and scratching will go on incessantly. The puppy should be free from umbilical and groin hernias, and the body should be plump without being pot-bellied, invariably a sign of round-worm; the puppies should be absolutely clear of worms.

The head should be full in skull, that is, viewed from the side the skull should rise in an outward curve from above the stop to the base of the skull. This is, of course, the ideal head; however, the poor skull will recede from the stop, and finish up as a flattish-headed type. The skull viewed full-face which ends in a peak at the top, may fill out at the temples, and again may not; the breeder will help you in this respect, but if possible choose a puppy with as much height and width above the eyes and a profile that does not begin by sloping away.

The eyes should be very dark at this age and set wide apart and square into the head; and even at this age they will be full of intelligence. Except in the really good head, the nose will more than likely not have gone back into line with the eyes, but this will take place as the puppy matures. The jaws should be wide and deep; in the perfect finish the lower teeth will just overlap the top ones, and the mouth have the lips just touching. I do not care for too long a line from nose to top of lips, this can give rather pendulous upper lips, which does spoil expression. Avoid a narrow, pinched muzzle; this rarely improves, and can be detected early in the very overshot mouth. If the muzzle should improve the result is usually a too strong lower jaw; that is, a rather bulldog thrust which is not pretty in a toy dog. Flesh-marking (pink marks) on the muzzle should be avoided. The finish of lips should be black, but if the puppy shows promise, and it is what you are looking for, I personally would chance the former, which appears only in the broken colours.

The ears should have a thin long leather, and lie close to the side of the face, a short rather thick leather may give a good ear fringe in due course, but the thin long one is the ideal.

Should you find a puppy with all these assets, it will be costly; however, reliable breeders will help you to find the puppy to fit your requirements and pocket.

A final word about the male puppy. If required for future show and stud, a male dog must be entire (i.e. both testicles descended into the scrotum) before he can be shown. All male puppies do not show this condition by three months, and should you choose a male at this age not yet entire for show, you would be advised to make some arrangement with the breeder should the puppy become a ' Monorchid '. If purchased as a pet this problem does not arise, as even if he were entire he is unlikely to become a show specimen. The bitch puppy purchased as a brood, or possible show, or both, will come in season from about nine to fifteen months. I would at no time consider breeding a bitch at her first season, unless this takes place after she is twelve months old, even so she would have to be fully mature if I were to do so. Sound strong stock will only come from sound mature parents.

FOUR

General Care and Accommodation

HAVING DECIDED to breed the King Charles, accommodation must now be considered. How are they to be kept? How much ground space, etc., can be given to them? and how much time can you yourself give daily?

Either you decide to keep your dogs as house dogs or kennel them. I cannot emphasise too strongly that these intelligent, charming little dogs should be with human beings, and nothing can suit them as well as living in the house with the family. Here, of course, the number of dogs depends on the space that can be allotted to them. The devotee will find room somehow for the number he or she wishes to keep. Kennelling at night does work; I have had to do this while house-hunting and living temporarily in other people's homes, when the dogs have spent the day in the house and garden with the family.

HOUSE ACCOMMODATION

This is simple with two or three bitches, as they will probably sleep together in one large basket in the kitchen – if they have not adopted one of the family and retire to bed with him! I am fortunate in having a house with three large kitchens, all heated. One 'houses' the stud dogs, another bitches 'in season' or in whelp, and the third, puppies. Puppies at resting time are kept in play-pens which are wired round, so that the adults are free to come and go. Puppies have their own playground away from the adult dogs. In one room is a large kitchen table, and a cupboard for medicines, shampoos, towels, and grooming equipment. The floors are quarry tiled, so that scrubbed daily everything is kept hygienic.

KENNELLING

I have used two types. One, a large stone-flagged dairy attached to the house. I had wooden kennels made to sleep two dogs and these were placed round the walls of the dairy. A large-sized oil heater was used and the whole place was kept beautifully warm through a bad winter, and puppies were able to play here when it was impossible for them to be outdoors. I have also used a large wooden building built as a workroom and play-room on concrete foundations; again with wooden kennels inside, and with heating in bad weather, it has made perfect sleeping quarters. I must again emphasise, however, that good kennelling and feeding alone is not sufficient; without human companionship the King Charles will not thrive. My dogs have always when kennelled at night been able to spend the day with the family.

All types of kennels must be kept scrupulously clean. I have always lined the wooden kennel with a good layer of newspaper, and a thick blanket washed and changed weekly. I do not like straw, it is rarely clean unless you know the source of supply and if it should be wet, the coat becomes stained. Blankets should be shaken daily, and in good weather hung in the air for a while.

FEEDING

Feeding is of great importance with the stud dog or brood bitch, show or pet, and each dog must be treated as an individual, and fed accordingly. Protein is the repairer of tissue while starch fills and keeps the body on the skeleton; but protein must be the main part of feeding. Protein consists of meat, eggs, fish, milk, cheese. Starch is bread and biscuit meal.

The only vitamins really needed by the dog are Vitamin 'B' found in yeast and wheat-germ, and Vitamin 'D' found in halibut liver oil or cod liver oil. If a dog is a country dog he will help himself to all the greenery he requires, and dogs do find the cellular substance of vegetables difficult to digest.

The town dog might benefit by a teaspoonful of well-cooked greens mixed with his dinner. Feeding today is expensive, and if you cannot afford to feed a dog or dogs well, do not keep one.

All my adult dogs are given two meals daily as follows:

Breakfast: which is a milk, vitamin and starch meal, consisting of a crushed shredded wheat, a heaped teaspoonful of Bemax, four drops of halibut liver oil and about a third of a pint of milk.

Dinner: which consists of two or three ounces (as required by the individual) of biscuit meal, or hard-baked wholemeal bread, or wholemeal bread unbaked, plus (according to size and appetite in an adult) four to six ounces of cooked beef, raw beef, fish with egg sauce, liver, kidney and paunch, rabbit or hare. Once a week liver, kidney and paunch is given; twice a week, raw beef, three days cooked beef, and the other days is varied with fish, or rabbit and hare, occasionally heart and tongue. Four yeast tablets are added to this meal. As with the human being a varied diet keeps the dog eager for his food.

Each dog should have his own bowl. Very quickly a dog will learn his place at meal time and go to the same spot daily. All cooking utensils and feeding utensils must be kept scrupulously clean. I like china bowls as they clean easily. Fresh water should be available at all times. I change this about three times daily, and the bowls should also be washed daily. It cannot be emphasised too strongly the necessity for cleanliness; where a number of dogs are kept many small illnesses can be kept at bay by hygienic methods.

I weigh all my dogs regularly, this is a great help, not only to see how a dog, especially a young one is doing, but illness can be indicated through loss of weight.

The King Charles being a very intelligent little dog, will learn a kennel routine very quickly. My dogs know where they fit into the daily routine, they know naturally their meal times, which do not vary, and they know their turn in the queue for grooming and they never allow one to change the order. They know when their turn comes for shopping trips, and sitting in the drawing-room, the younger ones learning from the older inhabitants.

The time comes when the puppy must commence his training on the lead. I find at about three months, it is a good idea to put a soft collar on for a short while daily, and later add a piece of string. During playtime, I sit on the floor or grass, the puppies play and climb over me, and I hold the cord; gradually they get used to the feel of this slight pull, and some take to the lead without more ado. Others take considerably longer, and patience will be required on both sides. Make the lesson as short as possible, and keep telling him what a good dog he is if he takes only a couple of pulls forward. It helps considerably to have an older dog with this type; my experience is that the shy retiring puppy takes to the lead much more quickly than the bold puppy, who throws himself about and really behaves like a wild colt.

Once he will accept the lead the time comes for training

for the show ring. The aim is to get your dog to trot along on a loose lead, showing his paces to the best advantage, and when standing to keep his attention so that he looks alert and happy. On no account 'top and tail', that is, holding up the head and tail as in some other breeds when showing. The King Charles Spaniel is a Toy dog, and as such he is judged. He will always look his best on a loose lead, watching his handler, and if possible wagging his tail. A happy confident King Charles in full coat is a real picture.

GROOMING

This is a daily 'must'; a quick comb through if no time for more, will help to keep the coat in order. Equipment required is a comb (I like a steel one) and a brush of the Maison Pearson type, and what is called a 'nit' comb. If you are a country dweller, and have animals and poultry within reach of the dog, this is an absolute necessity as the dog can pick up lice, fleas and ticks, especially in the summer months, and the use of this comb at grooming time will save the dogs and yourself a great deal of trouble. A dog does not have to be a dirty one to acquire parasites.

Everyone will adopt his own particular method of grooming. My own method is to:

(1) Brush the dog thoroughly with the brush. This removes any dust or loose hairs and stimulates the skin which is the greatest preventative against scurf, and encourages the growth of hair.

(2) Using a squeegie bottle filled with a coat dressing, or rain water which I find suitable, I spray the coat and ears, then I comb the coat all over until dry; this does not take long.

(3) With cotton wool rung out in Optrex, wipe the eyes, which being large and protruding, require cleaning. Use penicillin drops should they be required.

(4) Examine ears and clean if necessary.

(5) Wipe the mouth round with a solution of T.C.P.

(6) Examine nails, and trim if necessary.

These things do not take long; if every day your dog is gone over, the slightest thing wrong is immediately noticed, and action can be taken, saving possible suffering for the dog, and his owner's pocket.

THE BATH

During the summer months I bathe the dogs monthly, or more often if required; in winter when necessary, and according to the severity of the weather.

Use any good human hair shampoo, a soapless one preferably. A rubber spray-mixer is ideal for rinsing, and this ensures that the soap is really out of the coat. Rubber sprays are inexpensive and well worth having. Place a piece of cotton wool in each ear before bathing. Wet the coat, put on the shampoo, and rub well, rinse and repeat. Have ready a big warm towel, and remove the surplus water, do not rub. Dry with a hair dryer, or before the fire, squeezing out the water with a towel. Keep the coat straight by combing and combing; after bathing keep the dog in the same temperature for an hour and then give a brisk run.

I like to bathe the whole colours two or three days before showing, as this allows the oil to get back to the hair; the broken colours look their best bathed the day before showing. There are commercial dog shampoos on the market which are useful in the winter months; these do not require rinsings, which simplifies the bath, and the dog does not take cold.

FIVE

Breeding

I T I S N O T possible to go fully into this subject, as a whole book could be written on breeding alone, so I propose mainly to deal with line-breeding as being the most satis-factory way to obtain reasonable results. The pedigrees used illustrate this way of breeding, and are the main lines from which the show and broods of today have been built up since World War II.

Breeding is a long-term policy requiring a stout heart, quite a bit of capital, and a great deal of faith in your plan for producing a line of healthy, typical, pretty King Charles. The novice commences by purchasing a bitch puppy from a kennel (a) by correspondence accepting the breeder's choice and advice, or (b) by visiting a kennel and choosing a puppy that appeals to him.

Either way, with the puppy go her papers, the important one being the pedigree showing four or five generations. To the uninitiated this is just a list of names, possibly bespattered with a few or many champions, but other than appearing impressive, this is of little value if the purchaser has no knowledge of the dogs in the pedigree. A breeder will point out colours and information about the dog, and if visiting a kennel the purchaser can usually see some of the dogs behind the puppy. Most breeders are pleased to help the beginner to breed the puppy to the best advantage, and line breeding will in all likelihood be suggested.

The two most usual methods of breeding are :

1. In-breeding, recommended for only the most experienced breeder; for example, in-breeding is the mating of close relations, Mother, Son, Father, Daughter, Sister and Brother. To do this with success a full knowledge of every dog for at least four generations is required. Faults as well as assets will be doubled; this method is for the expert only who will know how to cull the result.

2. Line-breeding is usually understood to mean building a pedigree in which one individual appears repeatedly. It is not possible, however, to line-breed without also in-breeding to some extent, but it is not as close as in-breeding alone. The choice of objective in a strain is the responsibility of the breeders. Weaknesses, deformities, poor temperament will be obtained as well as the perfect points, also showing the necessity of knowing as much as possible about the dogs behind any puppy purchased with the object of breeding.

In following this programme, examine your puppies' pedigree and having been assured of one outstanding dog, still living when the bitch is ready, mate her to him. It is good to have some idea of the amount of influence which any animal in the pedigree may be expected to have on the offspring of a particular mating. The usual practical method in calculating is the assumption that each parent contributes one-half (50%) of the inheritance of each puppy, each grandparent 25% each, a great-grandparent 12.5%, and each great-great-grandparent 6.25%, and so on.

The influence of the dam is at least as great as that of the sire, so it can be seen that the saying 'a good dog will

MRS.
F. MITCHELL'S
CH. MICHAEL OF
LAVENDERWAY

MISS
VINCENT'S
PETER OF
VIHURST

MISS VINCENT'S
CH. FALAISE AND
CH. RUPERT OF
VIHURST

(right)
MRS. COOPER'S
CH. ROGER OF
LOUISDOR

(below)
MRS. CHISHOLM'S
CH. GOLDENDAYS
GALIARD ROSE OF
ST. LUCIA,
CH. WILDBOY OF
SANDYCUFT,
CH. GOLDENDAYS
GAY GALLIARD,
AND CH. PENN ROSE
OF ST. LUCIA

correct all the faults of a mediocre bitch ' is a fallacy. The strength of a breed lies in its bitches.

The following pedigrees illustrate line-breeding and show how the foundation lines of our post-war dogs were bred.

CHAMPION MICHAEL OF LAVENDERWAY

Bred by Mrs. Mitchell (who owned her first King Charles in 1903) Michael was a handsome Tricolour and has been responsible for a line of Champions. He had the ability to pass on his assets to his offspring, and we must view him as one of the corner-stones of the breed today.

PEDIGREE OF CHAMPION
MICHAEL OF LAVENDERWAY (TRICOLOUR)

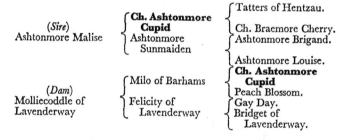

(Sire)
Ashtonmore Malise

Ch. Ashtonmore Cupid — Tatters of Hentzau. / Ch. Braemore Cherry.

Ashtonmore Sunmaiden — Ashtonmore Brigand. / Ashtonmore Louise.

(Dam)
Molliecoddle of Lavenderway

Milo of Barhams — **Ch. Ashtonmore Cupid** / Peach Blossom.

Felicity of Lavenderway — Gay Day. / Bridget of Lavenderway.

Ch. Michael is line-bred to Ch. Ashtonmore Cupid, an outstanding Blenheim of his day. Cupid was no chance breeding, but the uniting of two exquisite dogs, Tatters of Hentzau and Ch. Braemore Cherry, a Blenheim and Tri-colour respectively. Michael mated Lucille of Thatchend, sired Ch. Philemon of Thatchend, who in his turn sired Ch. Roger of Louisdor, the sire of Ch. Rebecca of Tonge-moor. Michael again mated to Koralo of St. Lucia sired Malcolm of St. Lucia, the sire of Ch. Wildboy of Sandy-cuft, who sired the most recent Champion, Juliana of Lavenderway.

Sarah of Esse was mated to Champion Michael, producing Ch. Mary Rose of St. Lucia. She in her turn was mated to Ch. Goldendays Gay Galliard, a grandson of Michael producing Ch. Goldendays Galliard Rose of St. Lucia. Ch. Goldendays Gay Galliard mated Sunmaid of Ilkleyview, a great-great-granddaughter of Michael, siring Goldendays Gay Venture now a champion. Gay Venture's pedigree (*below*) shows the strength of line-breeding to a dominant dog.

PEDIGREE OF CHAMPION
GOLDENDAYS GAY VENTURE (TRICOLOUR)

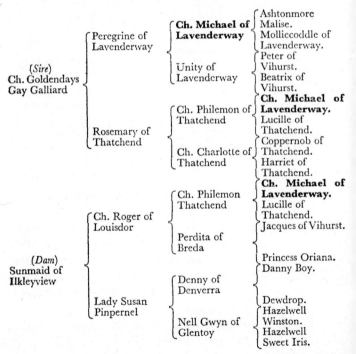

PETER OF VIHURST AND
BLUESHADOW HARMONY

Peter of Vihurst, bred by Miss Vincent, whose kennel was well-known in pre-war days, was prevented by the second World War from winning his third Challenge Certificate. He was a lightly-marked Blenheim, and like Michael, a dominant sire, a further corner-stone of the breed. Few

THE COMBINED PEDIGREES OF
PETER OF VIHURST (BLENHEIM)
(2 Challenge Certificates)

AND

BLUESHADOW HARMONY (TRICOLOUR)

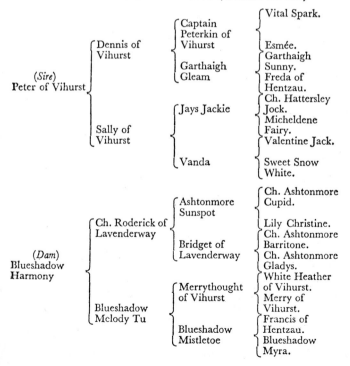

pedigrees are without his name; I have combined him with Blueshadow Harmony, bred by Mrs. White, another pre-war breeder, because the results of this happy union have had a deep influence on the breed.

The following five dogs are a result of this union, all dominant breeding stock.

(1) Ch. *Rupert of Vihurst,* mated to Carol Ann of Homehurst, sired Ch. Elizabeth of Homehurst. He was the grandsire of Ch. Clarissa of St. Lucia. Ch. Pierre Again of Vihurst is line bred to this union through Ch. Rupert and his sister, *Vihurst Memory* (No. 2).

(3) Ch. *Hurlestone Peterson of Lavenderway* – mated to Melanie of Lavenderway a daughter of his brother Ch. Rupert, sired Cupid of Old Rowley, the sire of Shamus of Old Rowley, who when mated to Miranda of Poneke, a daughter of another brother – *Gouldesborough David* (No. 4) – sired Ch. Rapture of Oakridges (*see pedigree opposite*), a perfect-headed Tricolour Dog, now in America.

(5) *Anthony of Breda* sired Ch. Gay of Breda (Sweden) and Ch. Antonia of Breda (Norwegian International Champion).

CH. PIERRE AGAIN OF VIHURST

A lightly marked Blenheim, bred by Miss Vincent and generally acknowledged to be the most outstanding King Charles on the show bench today. He won his 21st Challenge Certificate, and was best of breed at Crufts last year (1959) at the age of 10 years. To handle Pierre is a lesson in how a King Charles body should be constructed. Pierre is line bred to the Peter of Vihurst – Blueshadow Harmony combination and again doubled-up to Peter alone.

In passing you will notice (*see pedigree on p. 38*) that Ch. Jasper of Lavenderway, bred by Mrs. Mitchell and owned by Mrs. Pond, is half-brother to Ch. Michael of Lavenderway through Molliecoddle of Lavenderway, thus

PEDIGREE OF CHAMPION
RAPTURE OF OAKRIDGES (TRICOLOUR)
(Junior Warrant)

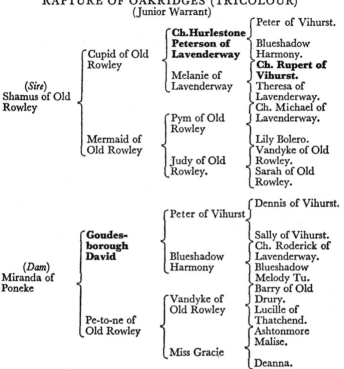

illustrating the strength of a breed in its bitches. Ch. Jasper like his half brother had the ability to pass on quality and mated to Penelope of Breda, sired Champions Celia of Breda, Osbaston Jeanette of Breda, Serena and Glazbert Troubadour.

The Black and Tans and Rubys were rather more neglected after the second World War than were the broken colours. There are more about at the present time, but the quality generally does not compare with the broken colours although where they are good the comparison is very favour-

PEDIGREE OF CHAMPION
PIERRE AGAIN OF VIHURST (BLENHEIM)
(21 Challenge Certificates)

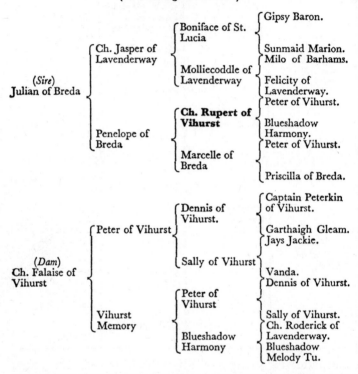

(Sire) Julian of Breda	Ch. Jasper of Lavenderway	Boniface of St. Lucia	Gipsy Baron.
			Sunmaid Marion.
		Molliecoddle of Lavenderway	Milo of Barhams.
			Felicity of Lavenderway.
	Penelope of Breda	**Ch. Rupert of Vihurst**	Peter of Vihurst.
			Blueshadow Harmony.
		Marcelle of Breda	Peter of Vihurst.
			Priscilla of Breda.
(Dam) Ch. Falaise of Vihurst	Peter of Vihurst	Dennis of Vihurst.	Captain Peterkin of Vihurst.
			Garthaigh Gleam.
		Sally of Vihurst	Jays Jackie.
			Vanda.
	Vihurst Memory	Peter of Vihurst	Dennis of Vihurst.
			Sally of Vihurst.
		Blueshadow Harmony	Ch. Roderick of Lavenderway.
			Blueshadow Melody Tu.

able. Mrs. White bred Blue-Shadow Black Billy, a black and tan grandson of Minasters Jolly Roger (bred by Mr. Whiting who was very well known for his whole colours in pre-war days) and line bred to the well known pre-war Ch. Little Minaster. Black Billy mated to War Declared sired Rupert of Grenewich and Hunter's Affidavit, both black and tans. These two dogs are the foundation post-war sires and bred as follows :

PEDIGREE OF
RUPERT OF GRENEWICH (BLACK AND TAN)

			Minasters Jolly Roger.
(Sire) Blueshadow Black Billy	Minasters Merry Andrew		Miss Carmen.
	Blueshadow Merry Maiden	Minasters Jolly Roger.	
		Blueshadow Marvel.	
(Dam) War Declared	Golden Surprise	Golden Pippin.	
		Lovely.	
	Miss Romance	Golden Pippin.	
		Dainty.	

PEDIGREE OF ROBIN OF OAKRIDGES (RUBY)
(2 Challenge Certificates)

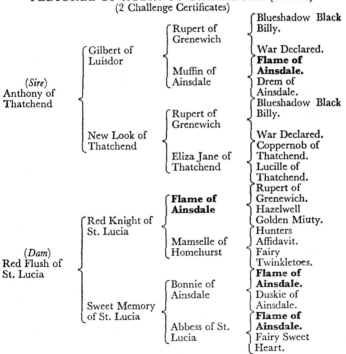

(Sire) Anthony of Thatchend	Gilbert of Luisdor	Rupert of Grenewich	Blueshadow Black Billy.
			War Declared.
		Muffin of Ainsdale	**Flame of Ainsdale.**
			Drem of Ainsdale.
	New Look of Thatchend	Rupert of Grenewich	Blueshadow Black Billy.
			War Declared.
		Eliza Jane of Thatchend	Coppernob of Thatchend.
			Lucille of Thatchend.
(Dam) Red Flush of St. Lucia	Red Knight of St. Lucia	**Flame of Ainsdale**	Rupert of Grenewich.
			Hazelwell Golden Miuty.
		Mamselle of Homehurst	Hunters Affidavit.
			Fairy Twinkletoes.
	Sweet Memory of St. Lucia	Bonnie of Ainsdale	**Flame of Ainsdale.**
			Duskie of Ainsdale.
		Abbess of St. Lucia	**Flame of Ainsdale.**
			Fairy Sweet Heart.

Hunters Affidavit mated to Fairy Twinkletoes, sired Byng Boy of Breda for Mrs. Pond, and Mamselle of Homehurst for Mrs. Jackson. Rupert of Grenewich mated to Hazelwell Minty, sired Flame of Ainsdale, a Ruby, for Mrs. Hawkes and to Muffin of Ainsdale sired Gilbert of Louisdor, a Black and Tan for Miss Walker. Flame and Gilbert being the whole-colour cornerstones of the breed. Flame mated to Mamselle sired Red Knight of St. Lucia, the sire of Gold Sunset of St. Lucia, who in his turn, mated to Gilbertina of Thatchend, Gilbert's daughter, sired Sirius of St. Lucia, winner of 1 Challenge Certificate.

Gold Sunset's sister, Red Flush of St. Lucia, mated to Anthony of Thatchend (holder of one Challenge Certificate) a son of Gilbert, sired Robin of Oakridges, the holder of two Challenge Certificates (see pedigree p. 39).

Gilbert of Louisdor held three Reserve Challenge Certificates. I mated him to his granddaughter Bunty of Zubaida, and he sired Zepherine Black Knight (unshown) and Zepherine Pink Rose, a small Ruby bitch of great quality whose show career was ended through an unfortunate accident. The pedigree of her son (see opposite), Zepherine Grenadier (Black and Tan) shows a further example of line breeding to a dominant dog.

Ch. Noranette, a Black and Tan bitch owned by Mrs. Holme and bred by Mrs. Cuthbert in 1936, was the first post-war whole colour champion. She took her first Challenge Certificate in 1939; the war years intervened and in 1946 at ten years of age, she took her second and the following year when eleven, became a Champion. This achievement is proof of the King Charles lasting powers. Noranette was bred the same way as Blueshadow Black Billy. Her pedigree (see p. 42) is a further example of line-breeding.

Photographs are not available for all the dogs under discussion, but those that are show King Charles Spaniels

*Valevan puppy : Blenheim King
Charles Spaniel*

Colour photos by Anne Cumbers

*Eight month old Ruby (rarest
colour) King Charles Spaniel :
Huntglen Red Sorrel*

Tricolour King Charles Spaniel puppy : Huntglen Barvae Domino : bred by Mrs. Gladys Clayton

Puppies in puppy pen with windscreen : bred by Mrs. Horton

Ch. Winston Evans of Maxholt

*Tricolour Blenheim King
Charles Spaniel puppies:
Huntglen Barvae Domino and
Huntglen Barue Digby: bred
by Mrs. Clayton*

Black and tan King Charles Spaniel: Ch. Huntglen Black Narcissus:
bred by Mrs. Harper

Tricolour Valevan King Charles Spaniel puppy

PEDIGREE OF
ZEPHERINE GRENADIER (BLACK AND TAN)
7. Months' Puppy

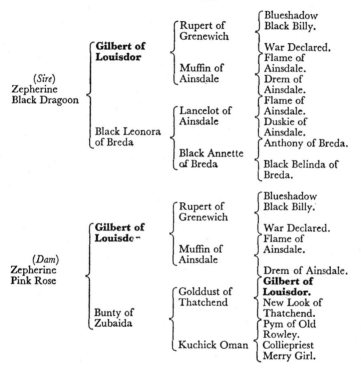

(Sire) Zepherine Black Dragoon	**Gilbert of Louisdor**	Rupert of Grenewich	Blueshadow Black Billy. War Declared.
		Muffin of Ainsdale	Flame of Ainsdale. Drem of Ainsdale.
	Black Leonora of Breda	Lancelot of Ainsdale	Flame of Ainsdale. Duskie of Ainsdale.
		Black Annette of Breda	Anthony of Breda. Black Belinda of Breda.
(Dam) Zepherine Pink Rose	**Gilbert of Louisdor**	Rupert of Grenewich	Blueshadow Black Billy. War Declared.
		Muffin of Ainsdale	Flame of Ainsdale. Drem of Ainsdale.
	Bunty of Zubaida	Golddust of Thatchend	**Gilbert of Louisdor.** New Look of Thatchend.
		Kuchick Oman	Pym of Old Rowley. Colliepriest Merry Girl.

that have considered breeding behind them and are typical of what we should all be aiming at. In a book of this size, space is limited and examples of poor specimens have had to give way to photographs of good ones. As this book is mainly to help and encourage the novice to the breed I decided, again because of space, to use illustrations of dogs that appear in most modern pedigrees, rather than post-war dogs, however beautiful. Thus when reading about and seeing the dogs behind your puppy the pedigree would

PEDIGREE OF CHAMPION
NORANETTE (BLACK AND TAN)

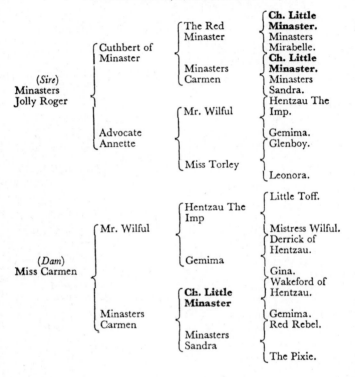

become more of a reality than just a string of names, and perhaps you will be enthused and decide to join the devotees of the King Charles Spaniel.

Year	Name of Dog	Owner	Breeder	Qualified
1946	—	—	—	—
1947	Blueshadow Romona Ch. ..	Mrs. D. E. White	Owner ..	Sept. '47
	Hunters Golden Pippin Ch. ..	Mrs. S. A. Knight	Owner ..	Sept. '47
	Michael of Lavenderway Ch.	Mrs. E. H. Mitchell ..	Owner ..	Nov. '47
	Noranette Ch.	Mrs. D. V. Holme ..	Mrs. A. Cuthbert ..	April '47
1948	Delysia of Lavenderway Ch.	Mr. J. W. Weston ..	Owner ..	April '48
	Falaise of Vihurst Ch. ..	Miss D. V. Vincent ..	Owner ..	Oct. '48
	Gouldesbrough Merlyn Ch.	Mrs. B. M. Kemp ..	Mrs. D. E. White	Oct. '48
	Rupert of Vihurst Ch. ..	Miss D. V. Vincent ..	Mrs. D. E. White	July '48
1949	Hurlstone Peterson of Lavenderway Ch.	Mr. J. W. Weston ..	Mrs. D. E. White ..	Nov. '49
	Philemon of Thatchend Ch. ..	Mrs. W. A. Darrocott	Owner ..	Feb. '49
	Sandroy Rhona Ch. ..	Mr. H. Hough ..	Mrs. D. E. White ..	Feb. '49
1950	Charlotte of Thatchend Ch.	Mrs. W. A. Darracott	Owner ..	Mar. '50
	Crispin of Lavenderway Ch.	Mrs. E. H. Mitchell ..	Owner ..	Nov. '50
	Denverra Dainty Boy Ch. ..	Mrs. S. R. Chatwin	Owner ..	July '50
	Lydia of Lavenderway Ch. ..	Mrs. E. H. Mitchell ..	Owner ..	April '50
	Pennant of Paxina Ch. ..	Miss I. N. Abbott ..	Owner ..	Aug. '50
	Serena of Breda Ch. ..	Dr. W. Clement ..	Mrs. E. Pond ..	April '50
1951	Betty of Hatherleigh Ch. ..	Mrs. M. Castle ..	Mrs. F. Dalton	Mar. '51
	Elizabeth of Homehurst Ch.	Mrs. D. V. Jackson ..	Owner ..	Nov. '51
	Jasper of Lavenderway Ch.	Mrs. V. E. Pond ..	Mrs. E. H. Mitchell ..	Sept. '51
	Joy of Vihurst Ch.	Miss D. V. Vincent ..	Owner ..	April '51
	Osbaston Jeannette of Breda Ch. ..	Mrs. A. Henderson	Mrs. V. E. Pond ..	Sept. '51
1952	Celia of Breda Ch.	Mrs. V. E. Pond	Owner ..	Feb. '52

POST-WAR CHAMPIONS *(contd.)*

Year	Name of Dog	Owner	Breeder	Qualified
1952	Pierre Again of Vihurst Ch.	Miss D. V. Vincent ..	Owner	Nov. '52
	Roger of Louisdor Ch.	Mrs. M. Cooper ..	Miss M. B. Walker ..	Mar. '52
	Sandycuft Julian of St. Lucia Ch.	Mr. J. Weston	Mrs. M. E. Gristwood	Sept. '52
1953	Cordelia of Lavenderway Ch.	Mrs. E. H. Mitchell ..	Owner	July '53
	Mary Rose of St. Lucia Ch.	Mrs. M. E. Gristwood	Mrs. K. Moger	April '53
	Miranda of Lavenderway Ch.	Mrs. E. H. Mitchell ..	Owner	Sept. '53
	Sweet Memory of Oakridges Ch.	Mrs. J. S. Castle	Owner	Mar. '53
	Troubadour of Glazert Ch.	Dr. W. Clement	Mrs. V. E. Pond	Sept. '53
1954	Alexandra of Thatchend Ch.	Mrs. M. E. Gristwood	Mrs. W. A. Darracott	Nov. '54
	Little Sir John Ch.	Mr. H. Hough ..	Owner	May '54
1955	Clarissa of St. Lucia Ch.	Mrs. M. E. Gristwood	Mrs. F. Mitchell	Mar. '55
	Goldendays Gay Galliard Ch.	Mrs. E. C. H. Chisholm	Owner	Mar. '55
	Hunters Black Magic Ch. ..	Mr. H. Hough ..	Mrs. S. A. Knight	Dec. '55
1956	Goldendays Galiard Rose of St. Lucia Ch.	Mrs. E. C. H. Chisholm	Mrs. M. E. Gristwood	Sept. '56
	Goldendays Penn Rose of St. Lucia Ch.	Mrs. E. C. H. Chisholm	Mrs. M. E. Gristwood	April '56
	Lovely Memory of Oakridges Ch.	Mrs. J. S. Castle ..	Owner	June '56
	Wildboy of Sandycuft Ch.	Mrs. E. C. H. Chisholm	Mrs. N. M. Alexander	Dec. '56
1957	—	—	—	—
1958	Rebecca of Tongemoor Ch. ..	Mr. E. Hulme ..	Mrs. M. Cooper	Apr. '58
	Rapture of Oakridges Ch.	Mrs. J. S. Castle ..	Owner	Mar. '58
1959	Juliana of Lavenderway Ch.	Mrs. D. E. White	Mrs. E. H. Mitchell ..	Feb. '59
	Goldendays Gay Venture Ch.	Mrs. E. C. H. Chisholm	Owner	May '59

SIX

The Stud Dog

WHAT QUALITIES are looked for in the Stud Dog?
First and foremost he must be impeccably bred, and have
no outstanding fault such as poor hind action, bad mouth,
light eyes which he could pass on to his offspring, and of
course he must be entire. Supposing you have a nice young-
ster coming along who answers to the above qualifications,
the next thing is to introduce him to stud work. Providing,
and the emphasis is on this provision, the young dog is
mature, both physically and mentally at ten months, it is
very worth while introducing him to his first bitch. A young
dog is easier to train the way you want him. Choose a
matron who is gentle and easy to mate, and commence
as you intend to go on. Teach your trainee that every bitch
he is expected to mate will be held for him, in this way all
the frustration of chasing and becoming exhausted is by-
passed, and the dog appreciates the fact that his job is
made easier for him. Once he has mated his first bitch this
way he will have full confidence in you (the handler), and
future matings, even difficult ones, will be overcome together. Always talk to the dogs, they like to know they are
pleasing. Should you not succeed at this first attempt, in all

probability your dog is not yet ready, so keep trying him whenever you have a suitable bitch. After this first mating do not use him again for about three months. Gradually introduced to stud work means that your dog will not get bored or his progeny lose virility.

If you intend to do stud work, you must have suitable accommodation for the visitors, and one hundred per cent care must be given to them. Always examine the bitch on arrival to make sure her skin is healthy and free from parasites; this is only a minute's work but can save what may be weeks of trouble. Fleas, lice and skin troubles are easier to acquire than get rid of. The King Charles is by nature gentle, but at such times, and in strange surroundings, a bitch may behave in quite the opposite manner to what she does at home, and it is your job to make her feel at home and wanted. Talk to her, do not leave her alone for hours, the mating will be that much easier if she is relaxed and happy.

A bitch is usually ready from about the tenth day to about the fourteenth day; there are exceptions, some mating earlier, and some later.

You are advised to advertise your dog's services to approved bitches only. This means that you can refuse his services to bitches not suitable to his blood lines, or for some other reason. The stud fee is payable at the time of mating, and is due for the services of the dog, irrespective of whether puppies result. You may prefer to take a puppy instead of a fee. This should be set down in writing and signed by both parties, the sex of the puppy should be stated at the time. Should one puppy only result, the owner of the dog is entitled to it without question.

Neither the dog nor the bitch should be fed for some hours before mating.

Make sure first that the bitch is ready, examine the vulva (the female part) to see that she is physically ready. If hard, red, and swollen, with a watery red discharge, she is not yet ready. The vulva should be soft, and the 'lips' of the vulva opening, and either a very faint discharge or none at all.

Introduce the dog and bitch to each other, if absolutely ready they will be delighted to meet. They will strike attitudes and stamp feet, the love ritual; at this stage hold the bitch by her collar, or scruff of neck, leaving one hand free to adjust the vulva to enable the dog to penetrate more easily. When the dog manages to mate the bitch, hold her very firmly and as still as possible and steady the dog if necessary. When a tie is effected the dog will turn round off the bitch until they assume a back to back position, or you may have to assist him. It is not essential for this position to be taken up, some dogs prefer to slip their front legs to the ground and remain in that position. A tie may last from a few minutes to an hour. Remain holding the bitch, some remain passive, others will spend their time trying to get rid of the dog. Take care the dog is not hurt, by firmly holding the bitch.

When the dog and bitch separate, hold her on her back on your lap for a few minutes, then put her in an enclosed basket for an hour. A mating is occasionally effected and the dog slips out after a minute, i.e. without a tie; repeat again the following day, and keep the dog on the bitch's back for five minutes in case this is repeated. If the dog is prolific and fertile, a 'no-tie' mating usually gives as good a result as a tie. I have one bitch who has not tied to four different dogs, and she has had five puppies in every litter.

The question of one or two services arises. If the service is a good one and the bitch ready, I consider one mating is quite sufficient, provided the dog is used fairly regularly, but two matings should be given if asked to do so. We get considerable variation in size in our breed, also in length of leg, and it may be necessary to raise the dog or bitch. So have ready in your mating room a mat that can be folded up; a good thick bath mat is suitable, as it can be so easily laundered. A tin of vaseline is also necessary as this can make things so much easier for both parties, especially with maidens.

Your mating now successfully over, either wire or telephone the owner of the bitch informing her that she will be returning in twenty-four hours, giving time of train, etc. The owner of the stud dog should always be told the result of the mating for the kennel records.

MRS. WHITE'S
CH. JULIANA OF
LAVENDERWAY

Photo: Fall

MRS. CHISHOLM S
CH. GOLDENDAYS GAY
VENTURE

MRS. BIRCHALL'S
GILBERT OF LOUISDOR

MRS. BIRCHALL'S
ZEPHERINE PINK ROSE

MRS. BIRCHALL'S
ZEPHERINE GRENADIER

MRS. HOLME'S
CH. NORANETTE

MRS. CASTLE'S
CH. RAPTURE OF
OAKRIDGES

Photo: C. M. Cooke

MRS. GRISTWOOD'S
MR. GARRY OF
ST. LUCIA

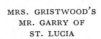

SEVEN

The Brood Bitch

HOW TRUE IS the adage 'the strength of a kennel lies in its bitches'. When purchasing a puppy or adult for breeding, buy the best you can afford, any bitch can be used for breeding, but only the good ones, again impeccably bred, will breed the good ones.

The brood must have no outstanding faults. I do not mind a suggestion of nose providing the muzzle has width and the jaw is not badly overshot, well-sprung ribs are not only correct for the breed, but are a must in a breeding bitch. I consider the majority of the present day King Charles are too long in the back, but try to choose a happy medium, neither too long nor too short. The ideal show bitch, who is really short-backed, can find whelping more difficult than the slightly longer backed bitch – room is required by growing whelps. Easy whelping is inclined to run in families, so enquire about the background in this respect.

A bitch can come in season any time from six months onwards, and then usually every following six months. My own experience is that some have their first season about nine months, others about twelve or thirteen months. Providing a bitch is fully mature in body and mentally adult to face a family, she can be mated at her first season if this occurs after she is a year old; a bitch of nine or ten months, even if a biggish one, is not ready for breeding. If she has not herself finished building her own body, and is forced to build a family and rear one, whàt possible hope has she of developing into a strong sound brood?

When the right time for mating draws near, and having decided to whom you would like to mate her, contact the owner of the stud dog in plenty of time; if a popular stud he may easily be booked, if left until the last minute.

The first signs of season will be a slight red discharge (which is slight or heavier according to the individual) from the vulva. The vulva will swell considerably, be hard to the touch, and reddish in colour especially in the broken colours. Note the day the discharge is first seen, a bitch is usually mateable from the tenth to the fifteenth day, but some are earlier and some later, so examine your bitch daily once the discharge pales in colour and the vulva begins to soften. It will then be noticed that the lips of the vulva open slightly and your bitch is now ready. If you own another bitch, you will see she is probably making advances to her, and she may now be tried to the stud dog.

Should you be unable to take the bitch yourself to the owner of the stud dog, and have to send her (in a basket) by train, do see, if the weather is cold, that she is warm enough, a woollen coat is comforting; at such a time the bitch will not be feeling at her best, and she will be a little anxious about being sent off alone, and warmth and comfort will do much to help her. Speak to the owner of the stud dog the day prior to sending, and give details of the journey, and if the bitch has any particular likes or dislikes about food, give these. Her hostess will want to make her feel at home. When she returns safely mated, make sure she does not have contact with another male dog until the season is over – usually three weeks in all. A final note – do see that your bitch is nicely groomed and absolutely free from insects before visiting.

EIGHT

Whelping and Puppy Rearing

AFTER MATING, the bitch should be kept in a fit, hard condition, and for the first five weeks, should be fed on her normal diet. From then onward her feeding must provide the essentials for her growing family, otherwise she will draw on her own supply and be in poor condition after whelping. Proteins should be increased, and starches reduced. Milk, meat, eggs and fish, with a little wholemeal bread, halibut liver oil and calcium should be given. Three meals a day are sufficient – I give one of cereal and milk, with halibut liver oil, and one crushed calcium lactate tablet, and one heaped teaspoonful of Bemax for breakfast. Scrambled or lightly boiled egg, or fish and egg and wholemeal bread at mid-day. Raw minced beef for the evening meal, with four yeast tablets. Fresh water should be available at all times as an in-whelp bitch gets very thirsty.

The period of gestation is sixty-three days; some bitches whelp from the sixtieth day, others go over. Never allow your bitch to go beyond the sixty-sixth day. It is well worth while for your Veterinary Surgeon to pay a visit if nothing has happened by the sixty-fifth day. This in-time visit may not only save your puppies, but your bitch as well, for if it should be necessary to perform a caesarian section, time is on everyone's side. Your bitch will not be exhausted, the puppies stand every chance of being alive, and you and your Veterinary Surgeon will not have to deal with an emergency possibly in the middle of the night.

Whelping is, however, usually accomplished fairly easily. It is usual for the temperature to be sub-normal for a few days prior to parturition, and usually rises a little afterwards, and providing it does not rise above 103° is all right. If you are used to taking temperatures, and it does not worry your bitch, a temperature check from the fifty-ninth day is an indication of what is happening.

The first signs of whelping, are often restlessness, panting and a general refusal of food usually preceding labour. This condition may go on for some hours before labour actually commences, much tearing up of the bed will probably take place. Keep your eye on the clock and make a note (on paper) of the time your bitch shows the first actual sign of straining (uterine contraction). No bitch should be allowed to strain for hours without some result; a Veterinary Surgeon should be called if after some time the bitch seems to be having unusual difficulty, or is showing signs of distress and anxiety. The experienced breeder can often do much to help the bitch herself, but the beginner is wise to play safe. The best whelping bedding is newspaper and plenty of it, replaced by clean warmed blankets after the whelping is over. The room should be really warm, and a basket with blankets, and a hot water bottle ready for the whelps. I cannot emphasise too strongly the need for warmth for new puppies; these little flat faced puppies just go ahead if they are kept really warm. A collection of puppies all huddled in a heap, are using up all their valuable mother's milk to keep warm, instead of using it to build their bodies. I use a thermostatically-controlled rod-heater under one side of the whelping basket.

After the first signs of straining (labour pains) you will find they begin to come more frequently until such time as the water-bag appears (which is a greyish coloured sac containing a brownish fluid, sometimes mistaken by the novice for a puppy). This is not always seen until the bitch is noticed to be busily cleaning up. Note the time of arrival of the bag; a puppy should be born within three hours of its appearance. If the bitch has been in labour and three hours passes and no puppy appears, send for the Veterinary Surgeon. Usually any time, from a few minutes to an hour or two, a puppy appears. It is enclosed in a sac, and in order that it may breathe, this sac must be opened. If the bitch makes no effort to do so, very gently break the sac and slip it over the head; the puppy will splutter, so clearing its mouth of mucus, and filling the lungs with air. Attached to the puppy by the cord is the placenta or after-birth; break this about one and a half inches from the body and remove the placenta. If the bitch eats these she only sicks them up again. The whelps will arrive as often feet first as head first. I dry each one as it appears and put it into the waiting basket until all have arrived. Once the family has arrived, take the bitch quickly out to relieve herself. She will not want to leave her family, but having relieved herself, she can then be settled down with her puppies. See that all can suck, and, after giving the bitch a bowl of warm milk and glucose, leave her to rest. The mother will nurse her puppies without any assistance for three to four weeks according to the number.

Any time from the third to the sixth day, the tails should be docked. Somewhere in the region of two-thirds should be removed, but try to judge (this comes with experience) the correct amount for each puppy. Dew claws should be removed at the same time, leaving a nice clean leg, and preventing much discomfort for the dog in later life.

Commence weaning at the end of the third week unless

there are only one or two puppies, when a further week is soon enough. The purpose of weaning is to get the puppies on to solid food. I have tried various methods over a period, and I have found the following seems to make a strong well-built puppy.

The First week of Weaning and the fourth of the puppies life. Give twice a day a piece of scraped beefsteak about the size of a small pea. The steak is scraped by placing it on a board and scraping with the edge of a silver spoon. This removes the soft flesh, leaving the fibrous tissue behind. The puppy takes to this much more readily than lapping milk, or one of the farinaceous foods, such as Farex.

The Second Week of Weaning. I introduce a milk meal, some puppies take more readily to milk and glucose, others to Farex and glucose, so common sense must be used. The meals offered are as follows:

> 9 a.m.   Milk meal (one teaspoonful)
> 12 p.m. Scraped beef
> 3 p.m.   Milk meal
> 6 p.m.   Milk meal
> 9 p.m.   Scraped beef.

Very quickly the puppies are looking for their meals; all stages should be taken slowly with them to prevent any upset, and the amounts increased gradually. A little crushed rusk can be added to one of the milk meals, and the yolk of an egg added to another. Gradually increase the meat until at eight weeks the puppies are having:

(1) Milk meal, Farex with a little crushed rusk or shredded wheat, Bemax, halibut liver oil (four drops) and half a crushed calcium lactate tablet.
(2) From half to one ounce of raw beef, finely minced, according to size.
(3) Milk and glucose.

(4) Half to one ounce of raw minced beef. One crushed yeast tablet.

(5) Small drink of milk last thing at night.

By three months, four meals are sufficient, consisting of :

(1) A milk meal as before.

(2) Scrambled egg and rusk, or, well cooked flaked fish and rusk; or one or two ounces of minced beef or cooked rabbit, etc.

(3) Milk and glucose.

(4) One or two ounces of minced beef with rusk or previously soaked biscuit meal.

I would emphasise that each dog must be treated as an individual, and fed accordingly. A small very active puppy will probably need more food than does the bigger, lazy one, so the foregoing is offered only as a suggestion. As the novice becomes more experienced, she will acquire methods of her own, but always remember that proteins are the body-builders and repairers of tissue; meat is the nearest protein to human and animal tissue, and will be therefore the natural food for the dog, and the one most easily assimilated, but the toy dog does seem to benefit and do well on a varied diet. Talk to your puppies, and speak their names from the beginning of weaning, and by the time they are out of the nest, they will answer to their names when called.

The next step is to register your puppies. We will assume you have a kennel name—my own, Zepherine, was taken from my favourite rose, Zepherine Drouhin (The Thornless Rose). The prefix is maintained by the payment of 10/6 per year, or by compounding for a lump sum, when it becomes your own property. Each puppy is registered with The Kennel Club for the sum of five shillings, and using your own prefix, add to it your puppy's name. All puppies should be registered, an unregistered dog is not acceptable for exhibiting, and naturally the puppies sell better if registered.

NINE

Hand Rearing Puppies

SOONER OR LATER you will in all likelihood have to rear the orphan, or give a supplementary feed to a family too big for a little mother. Let me say right away this is not difficult, requiring only time and patience. It is full of interest, and these puppies are most intelligent.

The ideal feeder is the Belcroy Premature Infant Feeder obtainable from any chemist at about three shillings and sixpence. When not in use this should, after washing, be stored in a bowl of cold water and covered with a clean cloth. Warmth and scrupulous cleanliness are the keys to success. A small carrying basket is ideal for the puppy, with a hot water bottle and soft blanket; from now on you are Mother. For the first twenty-four hours the milk mixture is easiest given with an eyedropper; once the puppy has acquired a taste for the food, he will quickly take to the Belcroy bottle. One of the milk mixtures listed at the end of the chapter should suit, but if this is not the case, I have successfully reared a puppy from the third day, on boiled water and glucose, and the juice squeezed from fresh steak or liver. He is now a mature dog with a beautiful body, so, never give up.

For the first week about half a teaspoonful of milk mixture must be given every two hours, day and night; after the feed the puppy must be made to urinate and evacuate. This is done by gently massaging the stomach and just stroking the tip of the penis or vulva with a piece of cotton wool. Dry the puppy with cotton wool, and dust the stomach with a baby dusting powder, refill the hot water bottle, and replace the puppy, making sure the blanket is dry.

The second week the amount of milk mixture can be increased to about a teaspoonful, and the last night meal can be given at midnight, and the next at six a.m.

The third week, increase the milk mixture and feed during the day every three hours; towards the end of this week introduce scraped beef as for the puppy being reared by its dam. Your puppy will be contented and grow apace if he is kept really warm, dry, and clean, and all the utensils, bedding, etc. are kept as they would be for a human baby. These little orphans literally jump and shout for joy as they get older whenever they hear their foster mother's voice – such wonderful compensation.

Baby milks such as ' Ostermilk ' etc. can be and are successfully used but I have myself had the best results with one of the following mixtures.

Half milk, half water and glucose.	Half milk, half water and Virol.	Half milk, half water and raw egg yolk.
For example—	For example—	For example—
1 tsp. milk	1 tsp. milk	1 tsp. milk
1 tsp. water	1 tsp. water	1 tsp. water
$\frac{1}{4}$ tsp. glucose.	$\frac{1}{8}$ tsp. Virol.	$\frac{1}{8}$ tsp. raw egg yolk.

Regular weekly weighing is essential to see the puppy is putting on weight correctly, this is very like the human baby, the same amount will be put on regularly week by week.

TEN

Choosing the "In Nest" Puppy

THE KING CHARLES SPANIEL, being a very slow developer, is one of the most difficult breeds to pick in the nest, but once you have seen a good one from birth, you have absolutely no doubts about how it will turn out, but this type is rare. The difficulty comes in picking the best from the general run of puppies born, and there will be puppies who will reach champion status amongst these.

Look well at puppies about twenty-four hours after birth, the best will be the one or ones who have the roundest possible heads, with already a short nose with possibly a lumpy ridge above it. Ones with what I can only describe as having 'Roman' noses viewed in profile will be the normal run in puppies. The line of eye in the first type will invariably be set square to the head and the latter, slightly obliquely. Often the really round head, which is not common, will have a very kinked tail, but again I have met this tail on all types. The broken colours, and sometimes the Rubys, will be born with pink noses, these will begin to turn black after a day or two. Rubys and Blenheims are not born a deep chestnut-red; the colour deepens as they develop, and the real richness of colour comes with the changing of the puppy coat.

ELEVEN

Colour in Breeding

COLOUR IS A matter of pigmentation carried to the hair, fur, or feathers by the blood. Briefly there are three primary colours – Black, Chocolate, and Yellow, the varieties being dilutions from these primaries. These pigments appear in the hair, fur, or feathers, as various shaped granules, and the manner in which these granules are deposited has its effect on the colour produced. When closely packed the colour is dark, less tightly packed, lighter. In horses the black points (i.e. bays and browns) are dominant to the light points (i.e. chestnuts). Red cattle are recessive to black cattle. This also applies in dogs where the colours are comparatively pure.

Many colours in dogs seen today are man-made, therefore it becomes essential to breed for colour and markings as for other qualities. If this is not done, nature steps in and the artificial colouring disappears; e.g. pale noses and eyes appear if Blenheim and Rubys are bred to their own colours over a period. In varieties of spaniels (brown and white colouring) the standards give noses flesh coloured, eyes hazel to brown, as in the Clumber and Welsh spaniels. Where black colouring appears the points (nose, lips, eyes and rims) will be black and eyes dark, as black does appear to dominate other colours.

Our breed has four colours, the whole colours – Black and Tan, and Ruby, and the broken colours, the Blenheim and the Tricolour. Both the whole and broken colours have a dominant in the Black and Tan, and the Tricolour. The Black and Tan, speaking generally, is dominant to all the colours, and the Blenheim recessive to all the colours, but with the constant crossing, and hybridising in colour breeding it is possible for all varieties to appear in one litter.

If Black and Tan is continually bred to Black and Tan, the rich tan markings will fade to a putty colour, and white will appear on the chest and heads of some. This is because nature is taking over from man. Solid colours are man-made, nature gives to all so-called solids, a white flash, socks, and possibly chest markings, e.g. as in horses, cattle, and dogs not bred for colour. The same will apply to Ruby to Ruby breeding over a period, but the Ruby will also suffer by showing lack of pigment in eyes, nose and lips. The same will appear in the Blenheim to Blenheim matings. Tricolour to Tricolour matings will affect the Tricolours' asset of a well-broken coat; very dark heads appear, and loss of Tan.

Without doubt the best results are obtained from mating Black and Tan to Ruby, and Blenheim to Tricolour. The occasional mating of similar colours together then, does no harm; but one warning, if a dog has a light eye, and, or, poor pigmentation, however good otherwise, he will surely pass on these faults and they are almost impossible to breed out. The hybrid colours, i.e. Mismarked Black and Tans, and Rubys, having possibly white on head, chest or toes, should not be looked upon as outcasts by the serious breeder, as these are the planned result of mating a broken colour to a whole colour. The whole colours, being small in numbers, calls for the introduction of fresh blood, but this is not a matter of haphazard mating. For example, let us imagine that one has the ideal whole-coloured dog or bitch, with no suitable whole-colour mating and so one mates it to a Tricolour or Blenheim having the desired points which will enhance your line. Let us say four puppies are produced, two Black and Tans, and two Rubys, all with a small amount of white, on head, or chest, or both. Bitches from this mating, assuming they are in quality what one had hoped for, are most valuable, and should you have a Black and Tan bred male, a quick return to unmarked whole colours is obtained. A Black and Tan bred Ruby male, will throw possibly one or two slightly mismarked puppies, but also some unmarked ones. Alternatively these hybrids, or first colour crosses, may also be mated to a broken colour for their possible improvement. A mismarked Black and Tan mated to a Blenheim will produce, amongst some mismarked puppies, one or two Tricolours with rich tan markings, and plenty of it, sometimes lacking in the Tricolour today. A mismarked Ruby mated to a Tricolour will do the same, and mated to a Blenheim will produce one or two richly marked, excellently pigmented Blenheim puppies.

Selection in colour breeding is as essential as for other qualities, and to know the colours behind your dogs is as important as knowing the dogs. The following table gives at a glance the colour results which might be expected:

Black and Tan to Black and Tan:	All Black and Tan. If repeated over a period, white markings will appear.
Ruby to Ruby:	All Ruby, but if carried on, the same result as with Black and Tans.

Black and Tan to Ruby:	Some of both colours, unless the Black and Tan is Black and Tan bred, then usually all Black and Tans.
Blenheim to Blenheim:	All Blenheims.
Blenheim to Tricolour:	Some of both colours. Sometimes all Tricolours appear. If the colours behind the dogs are studied, it is usually found that the Tricolour is Tricolour bred.
Tricolour to Tricolour:	Usually all Tricolour, some very heavily marked, and not all with good tan. If Tricolours are Blenheim bred, a Blenheim can appear.
Black and Tan to Tricolour or Blenheim:	Mismarked Black and Tans, and mismarked Rubys. Very occasionally an unmarked Black and Tan, or Ruby.
Mismarked Black and Tan to Blenheim: Mismarked Ruby to Tricolour:	Some mismarked and some richly tanned Tricolours.
Mismarked Ruby to Blenheim:	Some mismarked, some Blenheims richly marked with good pigmentation.

I have used my own dogs for my colour experiments, and have never found broken colours mated to broken colours produce at any time a whole colour, even if carrying a Black and Tan in the pedigree. Lady Wentworth in her work on the breed also came to this conclusion.

TWELVE

Record Keeping

WHETHER YOU KEEP a dozen dogs, or only one or two, it is absolutely essential to keep a record of each dog. This can save a good deal of time and uncertainty should you wish to refer to a mating, whelping or any illness.

There are various methods. Kennel Record Books can be purchased in which all details are set out ready for completion. Personally, I like the Card Index system. I find it quick for reference, can be easily added to or discarded as one wishes. Each dog has its own card bearing its name, age, registration number, colour, sire and dam. If the dog is sold, the name and address of the new owner, together with the purchase price is entered on the card, and this is kept in the 'sale' compartment. If the dog remains, matings or whelpings according to sex are added to the card, as well as the number of puppies, colour and sex. Dates of 'in season', any illnesses, or any information appertaining to the particular individual should be entered. It is only a second's work to look up the record of any dog and to have a complete picture before one.

All dogs are weighed monthly. I keep two cards for this,

one for males and one for females. All are listed under their pet names, and weights after them, as this is inclined to fill up the 'personal' card too quickly. Epivax certificates are kept in the appropriate compartment. It is wise to ask your veterinary surgeon for a covering certificate for all stock Epivaxed, should you sell later. Pedigrees and Registration Cards all fit into their compartments. I also have a compartment for names. I jot down suitable names for future puppies when I think of them; they are then available when required, and crossed off as used. Licences, usually composite for a kennel, are also filed away. As you will appreciate, this is a simple method, and can be added to as one wishes. I also keep a filing box where Show reports can be kept in order, and a further one for photographic records of the dogs.

THIRTEEN

Showing

WITH THE EXCEPTION of the Championship shows listed, our breed is rarely catered for these days, but entries can be made in variety classes. Having decided to show, sent for and filled in your entry, the great day arrives.

Before entering the show ground the veterinary inspection must be gone through, this over, you are then free to go to the area that has been allotted to your breed. Toy dogs are benched in wire cages, and although these are thoroughly cleaned it does pay to cover the floor with newspapers; curtains not only improve the general appearance of the pen, but also keep out draughts. I favour plastic ones as these can so quickly be dipped, after the show, in disinfectant water, and wiped dry; a blanket or towel to match the curtains will be placed on top of the newspaper. Comb through the ears and fringes and put your exhibit in his pen where he will settle down and rest before the judging.

Find out as soon as you can where your ring for judging will be, and when this is likely to take place.

When the time arrives be at the ringside in good time. When your class is called, enter the ring; when the steward gives you your ring number, pin it where the judge and ringside audience will be able to clearly see it, and quietly wait your turn keeping your dog interested. Don't be too thrilled with your win, or too downcast with your loss and on no account query the Judge's placings. If you enter under a Judge, you do so presumably because you wish for that person's opinion on your dog, and so must accept the result. A Judge will often come to the bench afterwards and you can get an opinion then.

If you live a prescribed number of miles from the show, you will in all probability be allowed to leave early. An ' early removal pass ' has usually been issued for this; should you leave early without permission you may have to lose any wins you may have won.

Before mixing with your dogs change the shoes you have been wearing and thoroughly wash your hands. It is better to keep your show dogs away from un-epivaxed stock till they have been well disinfected; it is better to be safe than sorry.

FOURTEEN

Common Ailments

P R O V I D I N G   T H E   King Charles has been bred from healthy sound parents, and correctly reared, he is a healthy strong little dog, ready to enjoy life to the full, and suffers few ailments providing a few rules are remembered.

Wet feet and stomachs are the cause of many ailments in most breeds, so see that he is rubbed down when he comes in in wet weather, and watch eyes in the east winds. Having large round protruding eyes, the cold winds can start conjunctivitis, but if you are aware of this, and precautions taken, this will not cause trouble.

Treat your puppies and dogs as carefully as you would children, and be just as particular about hygiene at all times. An outstanding characteristic of the breed is stoicism; my experience is that they will stand great pain without a sound if the person they love and trust is beside them. A dog's normal temperature is about 101.5°. Up to 102° there is little to worry about, but above that a dog should be put into a warm room, apart from the others and the veterinary surgeon asked to call. A good veterinary surgeon is your dog's best friend.

ABSCESSES. These can form on any part of the body. If puppies' nails are neglected the dam may get a small puncture in the skin of the milk glands, and this can cause an abscess. If the anal gland has become neglected this is a further region for trouble, which is indicated by the swelling of the part affected, and a rise in temperature. Treated promptly the condition can be quickly relieved. Two injections of penicillin, bathing of the affected part, and dusting with a sulphonamide powder is usually all that is required.

ANAL GLAND. This is not an ailment, but when a dog is seen rubbing itself along the ground in a sitting position, it is often erroneously mistaken for suspected worms. The cause is irritation from the anus, and it is the anal gland that requires attention. The domesticated dog does not get a sufficiently constipating diet, and this gland does not get emptied with the bowel action. It is a simple operation and your veterinary surgeon will show you how to deal with this yourself.

BLADDER. Inflammation of the bladder or cystitis can be caused from keeping a dog too long without emptying his bladder, or may be caused by a chill, or exposure to damp. The dog may show no signs of difficulty when passing water, but blood may be seen mixed with the water. This can be quite frightening; again prompt action will quickly clear up the trouble, which will of course be dealt with by your veterinary surgeon.

BITES. Wasps and bees can be a real menace during the summer months, especially with puppies which delight in trying to catch them; stings can be frequent, and the shock can cause the death of a young puppy. Treat for shock immediately. I have found the best method is to pick up and comfort the patient; a little drink of milk or tea if available distracts the attention. If the swelling is just inside the folds of the lips, a liberal dusting of bicarbonate of soda quickly reduces the swelling, and a paste made from the powder, and applied to external stings does the same. Usually the patient is full of life by the time this has been attended to, but if he is still upset, give half a tablet of Disprin, and put him in his bed to rest. After a short while he will soon be all right. Stings in the eyes or throat call for the veterinary surgeon's aid.

COLDS. Flat-faced dogs are subject to these, but other than a little splashing from the nose, appear to suffer no ill effects. Plenty of fluids, and extra care if the weather is bad, will quickly clear up the trouble.

INTERDIGITAL CYSTS. These are common between the toes of the feet, usually caused by grit or other foreign bodies. This is a swelling filled with a fluid, and until this disperses, can cause great irritation. Bathing in a saline solution is of great assistance. The feet should be examined daily at grooming time, and all extraneous matter removed.

DIARRHOEA. This can be caused by too much, or the wrong kind of food, dirty dishes, worms or enteritis. Omit meat, and give farinaceous food and sponge-cake for twenty-four hours, together with sulphaguanidine tablets as directed by the veterinary surgeon. It is advisable to isolate the patient as diarrhoea can be infectious.

DISTEMPER AND HARD PAD. Immunisation against these diseases by inoculation known as Epivax, can be given from the age of nine weeks; it is to be highly recommended from this age. Future owners are pleased to buy a puppy already inoculated.

EARS. These should be examined daily, and treated by

whatever method your veterinary surgeon favours. If a King Charles' ears are examined regularly and kept clean they give little trouble.

EYES. These again if cared for give little trouble. Should an injury cause an ulcer, veterinary treatment is called for. If the eyes are examined at grooming time, anything untoward will be noticed. Cold winds cause a mild conjunctivitis, and penicillin eye drops or Dihydro Streptomycin drops used two or three times a day quickly put matters right. These are obtainable through your veterinary surgeon. Ingrowing eyelashes can cause irritation and watering eyes. If you can pluck out the offender do so. Thiazamide, an eye ointment containing a mild anaesthetic will ease the irritation, again obtained through your veterinary surgeon.

HERNIA. The umbilical and groin hernias are not uncommon. These are satisfactorily dealt with by surgery, and should not be neglected. Very small umbilicals usually disappear with maturity.

INSECTS. Fleas, lice, harvest bugs and ticks, can cause the dog a great deal of discomfort. A well managed kennel should not expect to have fleas and lice. If the dog is groomed daily and has hygienic living and sleeping quarters, these parasites should be non-existent. Dogs slept on straw would need as well as the daily grooming, a dusting once a week with a good insect powder such as Lorexane. The bedding also, should receive a liberal dusting. Ticks will usually let go of the dog if a piece of cotton wool well soaked in ammonia is applied over them. Should your dog be unlucky enough to pick up any fleas, lice, or harvest bugs (an infested visiting bitch can pass them on to your stud dog) the best method is to comb thoroughly with a 'nit' comb, and then bath in a good insecticidal shampoo.

TEETH. These should be examined frequently and any signs of excess tartar or decay dealt with by the veterinary surgeon.

WORMS. These are legion, but the round worm is the one mainly concerning the breeder. Puppies with worms, often have great appetites, but do not thrive. The stomach has a distended appearance, and the stool is often wet and unpleasant. Again be advised by your veterinary surgeon; Coopane, a veterinary product, is excellent. No starvation is required, and the puppy is in no way upset; if worms are present they will be passed within twenty-four hours. Worms are not a necessity; if your dogs are fed well on good food, and kept in hygienic conditions, worms in puppies are rare. Worming should be done about the eighth week, whether suspected or not.

THE MEDICINE AND EQUIPMENT CUPBOARD

This is an important factor in the kennel. The following will be found useful.

Brushes and combs
Nail clippers, scissors and tweezers
Coat dressing
Shampoos
Cotton wool
Optrex
Eye drops (penicillin)
T.C.P.
Dettol
Ear drops
Coopane (worm tablets)
'Belcroy' premature feeder
Eye-dropper
Virol
Glucose
Minadex (tonic)
Brands Essence
Bemax
Farex
Halibut liver oil
Yeast tablets
Insect powder (Lorexane)
Bottle of stomach medicine
Sulphaguanidine for bowel upset
Friars Balsam
Woolly coats
Blankets
Travelling baskets I store in an attic together with whelping baskets.

All these things are acquired slowly over the years; one starts very simply and builds up.

I find a kitchen cabinet ideal for storing the above. The drawers will take the brushes and combs, cotton wool, puppy towels, nail clippers, dog coats, etc. The shelving parts hold the Kennel Record Card Index, together with ' doggy cuttings ', etc. The medicines will fit into the shelves at the top of the cabinet, and everything is to hand.

Appendix

The Toy Spaniel Club was founded in 1885. The King Charles were classified as Toy Spaniels and further divided by colour as King Charles (black and tan), Ruby (red), Prince Charles (tricolour), Blenheim (red and white) and remained as such until 1923, when they all became King Charles Spaniels, divided as Black and Tan, Ruby, Tricolour and Blenheim, as we know them today. In America they are known as the English Toy Spaniels.

There are two breed clubs—

THE KING CHARLES SPANIEL CLUB.

President: Mrs. Hewitt Pitt.
Chairman: Mrs. Alan Henderson.
Secretary: Mrs. Kearns, 42 Kingscote Road, New Malden, Surrey.

The subscription is one guinea per annum, election is by sponsorship of two members. As a member you become eligible to compete where offered, for a variety of cups at the Club and other Championship shows. The committee and judges are elected by members by vote.

THE NORTHERN KING CHARLES SPANIEL CLUB.

Secretary: Mrs. Weston, 25 Butt Lane, Allesley, Coventry, Warwickshire.

CHALLENGE CERTIFICATES

There are ten pairs of Challenge Certificates per year, one pair being offered at each of the following shows:

(1) Crufts.
(2) Glasgow. Scottish Kennel Club.
(3) Manchester Dog Show Society.
(4) West of England Ladies' Kennel Society.
(5) Blackpool and District Canine Society.
(6) City of Birmingham Canine Association.
(7) Southern Canine Association.
(8) Richmond.
(9) Ladies' Kennel Association.
(10) Birmingham Dog Show Society.

ADVERTISING

Advertising plays an important part in the kennel programme; puppies must be sold to allow the Kennel to carry on, and advertising is the best way to do this. There are various methods, the most reasonable and possibly the most satisfactory is through the two dog journals, *Dog World* and *Our Dogs*. These have a wide sale at home and overseas. The local, or weekly paper usually has a livestock column. Some daily papers have a weekly column, but these are often very expensive; or there are weekly or monthly magazines. Very much depends on what you can afford to outlay. Should you live in a town, pet shops will usually display a card for you, with details of stock and your name and address. I have never tried this method myself, but I have often seen such notices displayed. I believe some small fee is charged should a puppy be sold through this medium.

BIBLIOGRAPHY

Lady Wentworth	*Toy Dogs*
Mrs. Raymond Mallock	*Toy Dogs*
Idestone	*The Dog*

Index